Plant Growth and Development

K12

Contents

Safety in the Science Classroom

Come to class prepared to learn.

Be responsible and stay safe.
- Follow directions.
- Be an alert observer: use eyes to look and ears to listen.
- Put materials away properly.
- Clean up after yourself.
- Throw materials away as directed.
- Tell the teacher if something breaks or spills.
- Ask for help when you need it.
- Report injuries immediately.
- Tell the teacher if you are not sure of procedures.

Be careful at all times.
- Use materials and tools carefully and as directed.
- Use goggles to protect your eyes, if necessary.
- Keep materials away from your mouth.
- Keep hands away from your mouth.
- Pour liquids carefully.
- Smell things by waving your hand over the container toward your nose (wafting). Never put your nose close to any substance to smell it.

Be courteous.
- Speak in a soft voice when others are working.
- Respect others and their need for space.

Plant Growth & Development

Did you read a book today? Have you worn a pair of blue jeans recently? Do you like to eat popcorn? All of these products, and many, many more, come from plants.

Plants and plant products surround you every day.

Almost every type of plant begins its life as a structure called a seed. In this lesson, you will learn about how plants grow from seeds. You will also learn about the role each part of a plant plays in helping plants meet their needs for air, food, water, and habitat.

Many Plants Grow from Seeds

Think about a tree in the park or the lettuce in your salad. Is it possible a tree grew from a seed as small as a paper clip? Could lettuce have grown from a seed the size of the point on your pencil?

Let's learn what's tucked in a seed and what seeds need to grow into the plants you can eat and trees you can climb.

These students are planting seedlings.

Experience

Plants: Alike but Different

This chrysanthemum plant has flowers.

Even though plants are different, we can find ways they are alike. If we take a close look at plants, we can find out more about them.

Work with your group. Look at these pictures of plants. Use your observation skills to look for specific plant parts, such as leaves, roots, stems, flowers, and fruits. We call these plant parts **organs**.

In what ways are all these plants alike? Talk about this with your group. Later, you will record your findings on the Plant Observation Sheet.

This tomato plant has flowers and fruit.

Experience

How Do Plant Organs Help Plants?

Animals and plants are living things. We need air, water, food, and the proper **habitat** to survive. The structure of an animal or plant helps it survive.

Even though we all look different, humans have the same basic body parts. And each body part has a specific job to do to keep us alive.

You have learned that plants also have basic parts: stems, leaves, flowers, fruits, and roots.

These are plant organs. We will explore how these organs help plants stay alive.

leaf

flower

fruit

stem

roots

Each plant organ has a job to do.

Let's Build a Plant Model

Materials

pipe cleaners

tissue paper

yarn

index cards

scissors

glue

tape

Models can be helpful tools in science. Today, you will work with a group to make a model of a plant and label the organs.

Procedures

1. Collect the materials.
2. Place the pipe cleaner into the middle of the index card. You want it to stand up.
3. Add yarn for the roots (below the card).
4. Add green tissue paper for leaves.
5. Use tissue paper for flowers.
6. Make labels on index cards for these plant parts: stem, roots, leaves, and flowers.

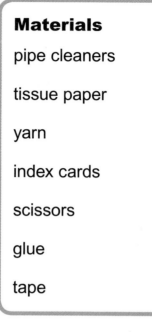

Build your own plant model using these materials.

Focus

Plant Organs and Life Cycles

You are now familiar with plant organs: stems, leaves, roots, flowers, and fruits. You know that each of these organs helps the plant survive. Each of these organs develops at some point in a plant's life cycle. Let's examine **life cycles** and when plant organs form.

From pea plants to oak trees, each plant begins life as a seed. A **seed** contains a plant **embryo**, or a small plant waiting to grow. The seed also contains a supply of food for the embryo.

Here are four early stages in the life of a bean plant.

Inside a Seed

Inside a seed there are two thick structures called **seed leaves**. Sometimes these store food. More often, when the plant bursts out of its seed, these seed leaves will capture sunlight and make food.

Look closely at this picture. Look at the parts of a seedling that have come out of the seed.

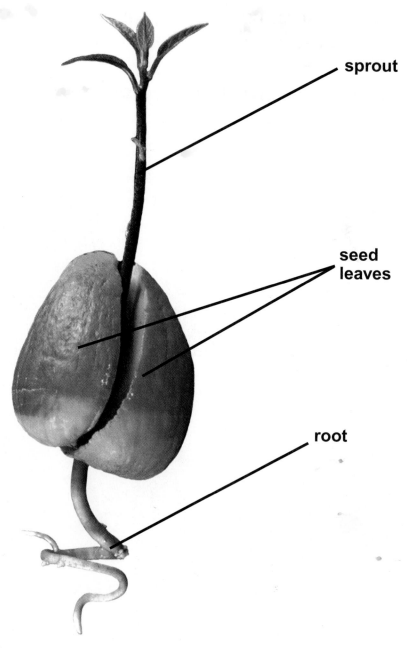

sprout

seed leaves

root

This avocado seed is sprouting.

Seeds Provide Protection

Seeds are strong and tough. They protect the embryo inside from cold weather and keep it from drying out.

Seeds remain tightly sealed until the right conditions exist in the environment. Seeds can remain tightly sealed for many years, as long as they stay cool and dry.

Usually, seeds need water, soil, and warm temperatures to open up so the roots, leaves, and stem can begin to grow.

The seed inside this acorn is sprouting.

This oak seedling will become an oak tree.

Here are five stages from seed to a young sunflower seedling.

Growing Up

Once it has sprouted, the young plant pushes its stem upright through the soil. The roots, stems, and leaves develop to mature size.

As the plant grows taller, it also makes more leaves. Its stem grows longer, and its roots grow deeper and wider. Soon, it will begin to develop flowers. Then the flowers will produce the **fruit**, which contain the seeds.

Start the Cycle Again!

A plant's flowers are the organs for plant reproduction. **Flowers** help a plant make new plants. A flower is necessary for the formation of new seeds.

At the base of the flower, there is a bulb-shaped part where seeds form. This part grows to form a fruit around the seeds.

You'll learn about the details of flowers and what they do in another lesson.

Pumpkin blossoms produce pumpkins.

Apple blossoms become apples.

Orange blossoms develop into oranges.

The Life Cycle of Plants

The length of time a plant needs to grow from seed to flower is different for different plants. Some, like the lima bean plant, go through this process in just a few weeks. Other plants, like oak trees, grow for about 20 to 50 years before they are ready to make flowers.

Some plants develop all the basic organs. Other plants do not. Some plants may not develop stems. Some plants, like cacti, may never develop broad green leaves. Other plants only have roots, flowers, and fruits. Plant life cycles are not all the same.

Spines on cacti are really leaves.

Mosses have no roots.

Aloe vera have almost no stems.

Think About It

Suppose you plant three groups of sunflower seeds in soil. You watch the seedlings grow, and then you place them in different conditions to investigate what happens.

Group A: Place seedlings in a sunny window, and water them daily.

Group B: Place seedlings in a dark closet, and water them daily.

Group C: Place seedlings in a sunny window, but do not water them.

Describe how each set of seedlings will respond to its specific conditions. Predict which group will grow best and tell why.

Sunflower seeds grown in the right conditions produce beautiful flowers.

Dr. Nadkarni peeks out from the top of the tree canopy.

Biography
Meet Dr. Nalini Nadkarni

Knowing about plants, their organs, and life cycles is very important to Dr. Nalini Nadkarni.

Dr. Nadkarni is a forest ecologist. An **ecologist** is a scientist who studies the relationship between living things and their environment. Dr. Nadkarni studies plants in rain forests.

Rain Forests

Rain forests are places where many interesting plants grow. Dr. Nadkarni often visits rain forests in Central and South America. She says, "I see many plants and animals that live only in the treetops. I want to know what is up there and what they are doing."

Dr. Nadkarni shoots a harness line to the top of a tree.

Into the Treetops

Dr. Nadkarni or another researcher is lifted into the canopy, sometimes 30 meters to46 meters in the air. That's as high as a 15-story building.

Once there, Dr. Nadkarni might stay a day or even overnight. She takes lunch or supplies with her. If she drops something or needs a snack, her assistant on the ground ties it to a rope, and Dr. Nadkarni pulls it up.

Dr. Nadkarni helps a student experience a ride in a climbing harness.

Understanding Plants

Dr. Nadkarni sometimes studies small plants that grow on tall trees high above the ground. Dr. Nadkarni studies the organs of these small plants and the host trees, or the trees that support the small plants.

Like all plants, these small plants begin as seeds and grow roots. Unlike most plants, the roots of these plants grow aboveground. Their roots grow on the trees that support them, but the roots have the same job as other plant roots. They gather nutrients and water for the rest of the plant.

In time, these plants grow stems and leaves. These parts of the plant gather sunlight for food and also transport water.

Dr. Nadkarni studies how these plants use their roots, leaves, and stems to survive. She studies how the plants share nutrients and water with the host trees that support them.

Dr. Nadkarni examines a specimen.

Important Questions and Answers

Dr. Nadkarni's work is very important. It helps answer important questions about how plants grow and live together in the rain forest. Even though she has been working in the rain forests for more than 20 years, Dr. Nadkarni continues to make new discoveries.

Tools of the Trade

Forest ecologists use compasses to find their way as they travel through the rain forest.

compass

climbing rope

Climbing ropes help scientists reach the treetops.

Experience

How Does the Stem Help a Plant?

The plant **stem** has some important jobs. The stem holds up the plant. The stem also connects the roots and leaves. But how does water get from the roots to the leaves?

That's a good question.

Let's investigate how water travels in a plant. Follow these steps.

Part 1 Procedures

1. Take a clear cup.
2. Put water in the cup (half-full).
3. Add 7 drops of food coloring to the water.
4. Place a celery stalk in the cup.
5. Predict what will happen over the next 24 hours.
6. Fill in the first four rows on the Stems Data Recording Sheet.

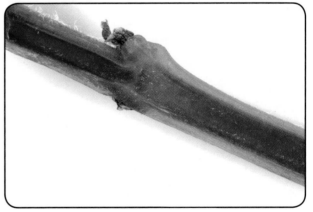

Water and nutrients travel up the stem to feed the plant.

Part 2 Procedures

1. Take a celery stalk.
2. Break it at both ends.
3. Observe the ends of the broken stalk.
4. Use the magnifying glass for a closer look.
5. Do you see how water might travel through the stalk?
6. Wait at least one day and observe the stalk again. Fill in the bottom two rows on the Stems Data Recording Sheet.

Experience

How Do Leaves Help Plants?

Look around outside. You'll see leaves everywhere. Even though they are different shapes and sizes, all these leaves have the same job. They make food for the plant. Unlike animals that eat plants or other animals, plants make their own food. They take in what they need and put it together to make food for the plant.

In this activity, you will investigate what happens to leaves in different conditions. You will predict how the plant will respond to these changes.

This microscopic photo shows one of the tiny pores called *stomata*.

The underside of a leaf is where tiny, microscopic pores exchange air and water.

Seeds Have a Complex Structure

A seed is a new plant. What will become a huge elm tree or a small carrot plant begins as a seed. Almost every plant around you came from a seed. Studying seeds gives you a sense of the power of plants and plant growth.

You'll be learning more about seeds in the activities that follow.

These students are planting carrot seeds.

Experience

What's Inside a Seed?

As you have learned, plants grow from **seeds**. The seed contains a young plant. When there is the right amount of water and sunlight, the young plant begins to grow.

peach seed

pepper seeds

Seeds may be different shapes and sizes. Some seeds, like beans, are larger. Others, like mustard seeds, are smaller. Seeds are different inside, too. As you study seeds, find out how they are alike and different.

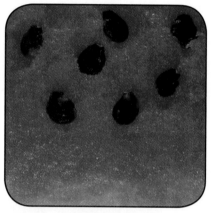

watermelon seeds

As a seed starts to grow, roots grow into the ground. The roots take up nutrients and water for the plant. The stem pushes above the ground. It grows taller and produces leaves.

Soon, the plant develops flowers. The flowers mature and produce seeds and fruit. Then, the cycle begins again.

avocado seed

Checkpoint
Review

Look at the two pictures here. At the top is a lima bean pod. At the bottom are acorns, a plant organ that contains the seed of an oak tree.

The bean pod and the acorn are each part of the **life cycle** of a plant.

What do we mean when we talk about a plant's life cycle?

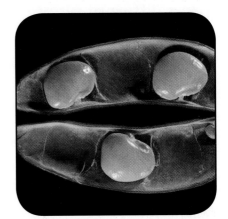

lima beans in the pod

acorns on an oak tree branch

How Does Your Garden Grow?

Look carefully at the diagram below. You'll see an experiment using three different plants.

Plant A is growing in a pot on the windowsill.

Plant B is growing in a pot on the windowsill, but the entire plant is covered with a dark plastic bag.

Plant C is growing in a pot on the windowsill, but the plant is bent over and the stem is broken.

All plants will receive an equal amount of water. Predict what the plants might look like after 2 weeks. Explain.

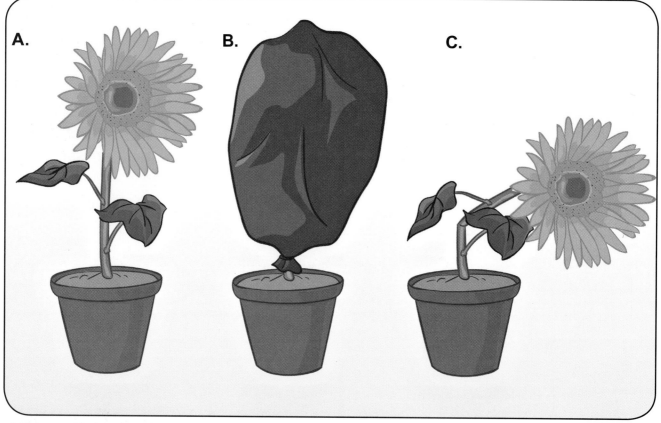

What will these plants look like after 2 weeks?

Life Cycle

The appearance of a plant changes throughout its life cycle. Which series of pictures below correctly shows the sequence of stages of a plant's life cycle?

A.

B.

C.

Which series is correct?

Seeds Germinate and Grow

Every growing season, plants emerge from seeds in the soil, pushing up their stems, developing leaves and flowers, and eventually producing fruit and seeds. The next growing season, seeds emerge again. It's a process that is repeated over and over, around the world.

In many plants, it takes months or years for seeds to grow and produce new seeds. We call this the plant's life cycle.

In the lesson ahead, you'll get to see nearly every step of the plant life cycle, in just a matter of days. That's because you'll be studying a special type of plant that completes its life cycle in just a few weeks.

With sunshine, nutrients from the soil, and water, seeds germinate and grow.

Experience
Let's Plant Seeds

Students plant a school garden.

We are going to plant *Brassica* seeds today. These plants grow and develop very quickly. *Brassica* plants belong to the cabbage and mustard family. A professor at the University of Wisconsin named Dr. Paul Williams developed these plants so students in the classroom could observe the entire life cycle of a plant in a short period of time.

What do you think will happen to these seeds after we plant them? What do we need to provide for these seeds?

Work with your group to follow these steps.

Plant the Seeds

Procedures

1. Cover the desktop with newsprint.
2. Gather seeds, planting quad, cup of soil, a cup of water, water mat and wicks, fertilizer pellets, and plant labels.
3. Dip the water mat into the water. The mat should be wet.
4. Put one wick into each section (or cell) of the quad. The tip should extend out the bottom.
5. Put soil into each section of the quad. Each one should be half full.
6. Add 2 to 3 fertilizer pellets to each section.
7. Add more soil and place 2 to 3 seeds into each section. Press the seeds gently into the soil.
8. Using the spoon or a pipette, sprinkle a little water over the soil.
9. Place the quad on top of the water mat. Set these on the tray.
10. Write the initials of each group member on the label. Place this into the quad.

Over time, observe what happens.

Experience
Thinning and Transplanting

When you plant a seed and it breaks out of its seed covering, we say the seed **germinates**. The seedling takes up space in the soil. The roots grow and take in water and nutrients from the soil. If there are too many seeds growing, they may not develop into healthy plants. You can discard some or put some of the seedlings into different containers. This is called **thinning** and **transplanting**.

Observe your container. If more than one seedling is growing in any one section of the quad, you need to thin them out.

too crowded

Follow these procedures for thinning.

1. Gently remove seedlings from the container.
2. Separate the roots of the seedlings.
3. If needed, carefully trim the roots with scissors.
4. Put one seedling back into the container.
5. Discard the extra seedlings OR transplant the seedlings.

Follow these procedures for transplanting.

thinned and transplanted

1. Put soil in another container.
2. Make a hole in the center with your finger.
3. Place one seedling into this hole.
4. Spoon dirt around the stem to hold it up.
5. Water the seedling.

Dr. Carver working in his laboratory

Biography
Meet Dr. George Washington Carver

When we think of plants, how they grow, and how we use them, one name always comes to mind—Dr. George Washington Carver. Dr. Carver was born in Missouri in 1864. He learned to read and write at home because there were no schools for him to attend. At that time, most schools did not accept African American students. When he was older, Dr. Carver went to college at Iowa State University.

Dr. Carver had little money during college. He had to work several jobs. He worked as a janitor and washed clothes for extra money. He also worked in local restaurants and as a trainer for the sports teams at the school.

Though he was quite busy, Dr. Carver did well in school. He was an excellent scientist and a sharp observer. He graduated from college in 1894.

Dr. Carver (center) with students

The Young Teacher

Dr. Carver became a scientist and a professor. He worked first at Iowa State University. Dr. Carver was in charge of the school's greenhouses, which are large glass structures where plants are grown. Dr. Carver studied how the plants grew and how their various parts functioned. One of Dr. Carver's fellow professors called him "a brilliant student, the best collector, and the best scientific observer I have ever known."

On to Tuskegee

In 1896, Dr. Carver was asked to teach at Tuskegee Institute in Alabama. Tuskegee Institute educated African American students. Dr. Carver knew how important education was, and he accepted the job. He started teaching at Tuskegee Institute in 1896. Dr. Carver's work there made him one of the most famous scientists in American history.

Dr. Carver was hired to teach at Tuskegee Institute by Booker T. Washington, who was a famous educator and an author. Washington was also a leader of African Americans.

Cotton Is King

At Tuskegee, Dr. Carver taught students and farmers about crops. He taught them how plants grow and about their different parts. One plant Dr. Carver focused on was cotton. The cotton plant was very valuable because it was used to make clothes.

However, Dr. Carver also noticed that the cotton plant sometimes caused problems. The cotton plant took a lot of nutrients from the soil. Growing too much cotton would leave the soil in poor condition.

Cotton needs lots of nutrients to grow.

Dr. Carver's research was of great help to farmers.

From Cotton to Peanuts

Dr. Carver thought that farmers should try to grow crops other than cotton. He knew that other crops would not damage the soil as much as cotton. Dr. Carver tried to find a crop that would be useful and less harmful to the soil.

Dr. Carver decided to focus on the peanut plant. He studied the peanut plant's growth and structure. He observed how the peanut plant did not hurt the soil the way cotton did.

The Peanut Plant

At the time, farmers rarely grew peanuts because they didn't think there were many uses for them. Dr. Carver wanted to show that there were many uses for the peanut plant. He began by studying the peanut plant very closely in his lab and in the fields of Alabama.

By studying the peanut plant, Dr. Carver learned many things. He learned the best time of year to plant the crop. He learned how deep in the soil to plant the peanut seed. He learned how long it takes the plant to produce peanuts.

The peanut plant's growing season lasts about five months. During the first two months, the plant grows to be about 46 centimeters tall and has leaves and small flowers. During the next three months, the peanut grows underground.

Peanut plants are an important crop for many farmers.

Crop Rotation Pays Off

Dr. Carver also learned how the leaves, the flowers, and the peanuts, which are the fruit of the plant, develop. He learned how these parts of the structure help the plant survive.

Most important, Dr. Carver learned that planting crops like peanuts could help return nutrients to the soil. He is given credit for the concept of crop rotation. With this method, different types of plants are grown in the same space, one type the first year, followed by another type the next year. Following this practice, farmers could grow cotton one year and peanuts or rice the next year without depleting nutrients from the soil. Some crops, like soybeans, help enrich the soil. Dr. Carver shared this important knowledge with his students.

Long grain rice or peanuts are rotated with cotton to restore nutrients to the soil.

Peanut Products

Learning about the life cycle and structure of the peanut plant enabled Dr. Carver to use the plant in many ways. He discovered more than 300 uses for the peanut plant. He learned how to make things like those shown below, plus paper, medicine, paint, and other food products from this plant. With these developments, Dr. Carver used his knowledge of science to improve society.

peanut butter

glycerin soap

rubber boots

paint

Dr. Carver is greeted by President Franklin D. Roosevelt.

The Wizard of Tuskegee

Dr. Carver's work also helped American farmers. His work turned peanut farming into a very good business. It also helped farmers rely less on cotton.

Dr. Carver earned the nickname "The Wizard of Tuskegee" as a result of his teaching and helping students and farmers at Tuskegee for many years. His work also earned him the respect of men and women around the world.

Experience
How Do Plants Change?

When we plant a seed in soil, we cannot see it. Soon, a seedling pokes up through the soil. The roots grow downward, and the stem grows upward. Leaves will form, too.

Today, you are going to observe and record the changes in your new plant. Be careful not to miss anything. Here are some questions to think about.

Where are the roots? Do you see the roots?
How tall is the stem?
How thick is the stem?
How long are the leaves?
How wide are the leaves?
Are the leaves all the same size?
How many leaves do you see?
What color are the leaves?
Do you see any flowers?
How many do you see?
What color are the flowers?
How big are the flowers?
What do the flowers look like?

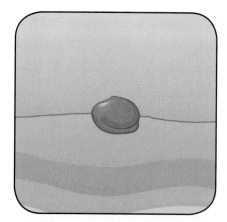

Brassica **develops from seed to seedling.**

Observing Change

Living things grow and change over time. We can observe changes in plants. When we observe plants, we can look for patterns of change. As we record data, we can watch for changes from day to day. This helps us understand plant development and life cycles.

seed

sprout

seedling

flower

fruit

The cycle flows from seed to sprout to seedling to flower, and finally to fruit, which contains new seeds.

Experience
Plant Development

Take a close look at the picture below. You can see a stem holding up the leaves. The "seed leaves" are still in the ground, providing food for the new plant. The "true leaves" are green and beginning to make new food using sunlight. Now, look at your plants. How do they compare to the picture below.

Look at your plants again. Do you see any flowers forming? Look closely. This is an important part of the plant's life cycle. Some of you may know what develops from flowers. If you said "seeds," you are right. Some plants also develop fruit that contains seeds.

Look for other changes in your plants. Watch to see how they respond to light and water.

true leaves

seed leaves

As this bean seed germinates, the true leaves open.

Focus

Parts of a Flower

Think about some flowers you know. Roses, carnations, sunflowers, and tulips are all flowers. Other plants, like grass and many trees, have flowers, too. If flowers look so different from each other, what do they have in common?

All flowers have the same function. Flowers are a plant's reproductive structure. Different parts of the flower play different roles in reproduction. Let's look closer at a flower to learn about the function of each part.

rose

tulip

grass flowers

linden tree flowers

poplar tree flower

apple tree flower

petal

sepal

The sepals and petals make the two outer rings of a flower.

The Structure of a Flower

It's helpful to think of a flower as made up of four groups of structures, one inside the other. The outermost is made of leaves called **sepals**. Sepals protect the flower while it develops. In some flowers, the sepals are green, like any other leaf. In others, the sepals are colored like petals.

Petals are leaf-shaped structures that surround the inner parts of a flower. Often, the petals are brightly colored and produce a scent. This helps attract insects and other animals that help the flower reproduce. You'll learn more about this next.

What's Inside?

Inside the petals, you'll find the flower's male and female structures. The first ring inside the petals include the male structures, called the **stamens**. Stamens produce a powdery substance called pollen, which contains male reproductive cells.

pistil

stamen

Looking Further

The innermost ring of the flower is the female structure, called the **pistil**.

Pollen from the male part of a flower lands on the pistil. This begins the process by which new seeds will form at the bottom of the pistil.

It is these seeds that will eventually land on the ground and grow into new plants. These plants will produce flowers, then seeds, and the life cycle repeats itself.

The pistil may look different, but it functions the same in all flowers.

Think About It

Flowers have special reproductive structures. Which statement describes what happens when a plant reproduces? Choose the best answer.

A. Stamens contain the flower petals.

B. Seeds form inside the pistil.

C. The pistil makes pollen for the plant.

D. Seeds are produced inside the stamen.

daylily

Ms. Mexia on an expedition

Biography
Meet Ms. Ynes Mexia

Ms. Ynes Mexia was a botanist, a person who studies plants. She was also a naturalist. A naturalist is someone who studies the plants and animals of the world.

Ms. Mexia was born in Washington, D.C., in 1870. However, she did not become interested in studying plants until she was 51 years old.

In 1921, she took her first botany class at the University of California. Her interest in the subject grew quickly.

Flower Expert

Ms. Mexia began going on trips to learn more about flowers and other plants. She visited different parts of the United States, as well as Mexico, Brazil, Peru, and Argentina. Ms. Mexia collected many samples of flowers and other plants on these trips.

Two of the flowers and plants that Ms. Mexia collected had never been studied before. One was similar to a daisy, and the other was a type of rust fungus. With other scientists, she learned about these new plants.

For example, Ms. Mexia learned how and where the plants grew. She learned how the plants flowered and reproduced. She learned these things by carefully observing the plants and recording her observations.

Here are some of the South American countries Ms. Mexia explored while collecting flowers and plants.

Ms. Mexia's Collections

Ynes Mexia went on major collecting trips for 13 years. She collected more than 145,000 different kinds of plants on her trips. Out of those many different kinds of plants, about 500 had not yet been discovered.

Ms. Mexia's work helped people learn a lot about the plants she collected. Her fellow scientists were able to learn about the parts and flowers of the plants, as well as how the plants reproduced. When she wasn't traveling, Ms. Mexia gave talks in San Francisco about her experiences collecting plants.

Ms. Mexia discovered flowers like these while on an expedition.

Ms. Mexia discovered a type of rust fungus that grows on plants.

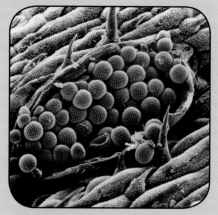

Look at this microscopic view of rust fungus.

Checkpoint

Review

The *Brassica* seeds you planted follow all the steps of a plant life cycle. You might not have seen all the steps yet, but soon, you will.

Which series of pictures below shows the stages in the *Brassica* life cycle in the correct order?

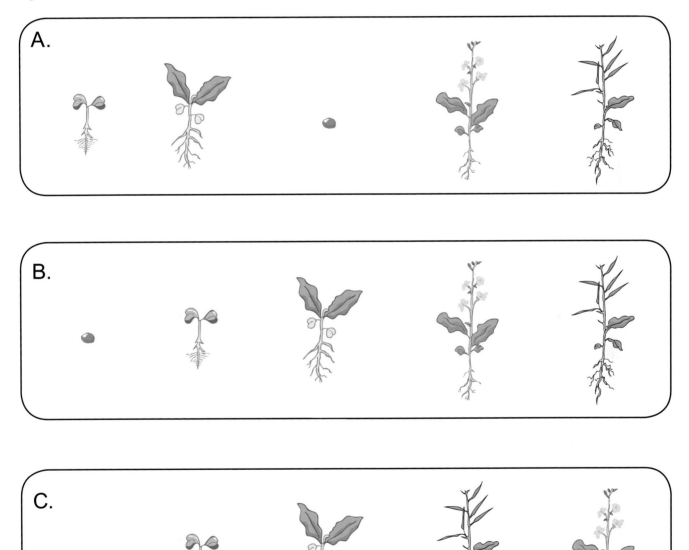

What Went Wrong?

You want to make sure your *Brassica* plants will grow. Following is a list of what you need to do. Some of these won't help your plants grow. Which should be removed from the list? Choose all that apply.

1. Plant seeds in potting soil.
2. Water plants once a week.
3. Keep plants under constant light.
4. Thin and transplant.
5. Put plants outside.
6. Add fertilizer.
7. Pick the flowers.

Nothing is growing.

Pick the Parts

Identify the main parts of the flower: pistil, petal, stamen, sepal.

A.

B.

C.

D.

The parts of the flower can be easily seen on this Madonna lily.

Plant and Animal Relationships

Close your eyes. Think of a beautiful flower. But wait. It's more than beautiful. A flower is a very important part of a plant. That's where seeds are made.

Believe it or not, insects and flowers need each other. Each one helps the other. If we observe them closely, we can find out how this works.

When insects and flowers get together, that's the beginning of new seeds.

Discovering plant and animal relationships is an adventure.

Experience
Design a Flower

Materials

construction paper

cupcake liner

pipe cleaners

yarn

straws

tissue paper

markers

crayons

glue

tape

scissors

Work with a group to make a model of a flowering plant. Use the labeled drawing and the artificial flower for reference. Be sure to show these flower parts on your three-dimensional model: roots, stem, leaves, sepal, pistil, stamen, and petals. Be creative! Make a beautiful flower, but remember to include the important parts.

After you make the plant and flower, label its parts: roots, stem, leaves, sepal, pistil, stamen, and petals. Later, you'll use this model for another activity. Be sure to put your name on the finished product.

Make a flower model of your own.

stag beetle

ladybug

Millions of Insects

More than a million… Hey! that's a big number. Did you know that there are more than a million different types of insects in the world? And they all have the same body plan. Let's look at the characteristics of insects.

First, think about your own body. You have a skeleton inside your body that protects your soft organs like your heart and lungs. An insect, however, has no bones inside its body. Instead, it has a hard outside covering called an *exoskeleton* that protects the insect's soft parts.

butterfly

praying mantis

More About Insects

An insect has three body sections. It has a head, thorax, and abdomen. An insect has six legs with joints that help it move around. Most insects have wings that help them fly.

For touching, smelling, and hearing, insects use two antennae on their heads. To see, insects have eyes. Some insects, but not all, have special compound eyes.

Now that you know more about insects, you also need to know that insects play an important role in plant reproduction. Let's learn how they partner with plants.

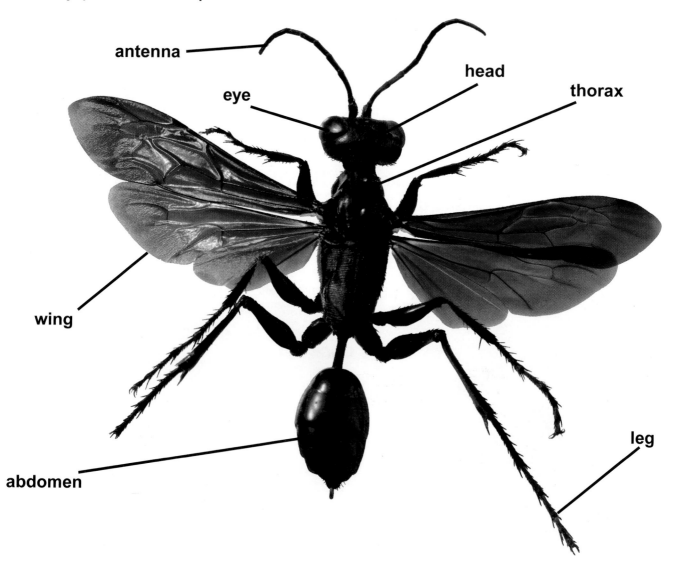

antenna

eye

head

thorax

wing

abdomen

leg

Experience

Invent an Insect

Materials

index card

pipe cleaners

wire (thin, insulated)

paper clips

pushpins

plastic wrap

wax paper

tissue paper

toothpicks

modeling clay

scissors

Insects are everywhere—all sorts of insects. Let's make an insect model. Remember to include the insect body parts that you learned about. Make your invented insect look real.

Procedure

1. Work in your group of four.
2. Talk about insects and their physical structures.
3. Make some choices about the insect you will make.
4. Complete the Insect Planner page.
5. Choose one student to gather materials.
6. Begin building your insect.
7. Write your names on the index card.
8. Add the name of the insect you made.
9. Place your insect on the card.

Great job! You are a successful insect inventor.

Bees carry pollen from flower to flower.

Those Buzzing Bees

You may have seen a bee buzzing around flowers. Thank that bee the next time you see another one. Here's why.

Bees are insects. Bees visit flowers. That's where they sip **nectar**, a sugary liquid bees eat for food. Something else happens when a bee lands on a flower. Tiny grains of **pollen** stick to the bee. Then, the bee flies off to land on another flower.

What happens next? You're right. Some of the pollen on the bee gets onto that flower. This is called **pollination**, which is the beginning of plant reproduction. After pollination, a new seed begins to develop.

Experience
Let's Hear It for Bees!

Today you will make a bee stick by gluing a dried bee onto the end of a craft stick. Be very careful, so you don't break the bee's tiny body. You will use this bee stick in the next activity. But first, allow the glue to dry completely.

Now, take a close-up look at a bee. Use a magnifying glass to examine the bee's body. You might be surprised at what you see.

Next, use a pencil and paper to make a large drawing of the bee. Include the three main body sections and some of the specialized body parts, such as the legs and wings. You might want to try drawing two different views of the bee, one looking at the bee from the top and another looking at the bee from the side.

Side view of a bee

Looking down at a bee

Bee coming in for a landing

Experience
Be a Bee

Materials

Brassica plants

bee stick

magnifying glasses

You learned that bees and other animals help move pollen from flower to flower. You are going to try doing this by hand in the classroom. When humans help transfer pollen from one flower to another, using their own hands, this is called *hand-pollination*. You can use your bee sticks to help with this task.

Procedure

1. Take two or more different plants with flowers.
2. Use the magnifying glass to look for pollen.
3. Rub your bee stick gently on a flower.
4. Look at the bee with the magnifying glass.
5. Find another flower. Rub the bee stick on that flower.
6. Use the magnifying glass to look for pollen.
7. Do you think you successfully hand-pollinated? How do you know?
8. Let other group members take a turn with the procedure.

Hand-pollinating orchid flowers

hand-pollination

Experience
Move That Pollen

In an earlier activity, you hand-pollinated your plants. In nature, pollination is accomplished when animals or wind move pollen from flower to flower. Some insects, like bees and butterflies, are well suited to pollination. They fly around and sip nectar at different flowers. Pollen sticks to their bodies and travels with them.

bumblebee

hummingbird

butterfly

Hummingbirds are also **pollinators**. The hummingbird's long beak reaches into flowers to collect nectar. While it is sipping, pollen gets on its body. As the hummingbird flies to other flowers for a drink, pollen travels along with it.

Of course, insects and hummingbirds benefit from the flowers. They need the sweet nectar. When living things depend on each other for what they need, we call this **interdependence**.

Focus

How Are Flowers Pollinated?

You've probably seen bees on a summer day, buzzing from flower to flower. Those bees are eating the nectar the flowers produce. In the process, the bees become dusted with pollen. When a bee travels from one flower to another, it transfers pollen from the stamen of one flower to the pistil of another. This step in plant reproduction—pollination—leads to the production of seeds. Pollination is very important to plants.

Bees aren't the only animals that pollinate flowers. Butterflies, birds, beetles, moths, and bats are pollinators, or animals that transfer pollen between flowers, too.

This bee is covered in pollen.

This colorful pansy has nectar guides that attract many insects.

These bright red flowers attract hummingbirds.

Look Over Here!

Some flowers display special patterns of color called **nectar guides**. The colored streaks or spots point to the middle of the flower where the nectar is located. Like lights on an airport runway, these nectar guides help pollinators locate a good landing spot.

Certain colors also attract different types of pollinators. For example, hummingbirds can mainly see the color red and so are attracted to many kinds of red flowers.

Day and Night

Some flowers attract pollinators that are active at night, like bats and moths. These flowers tend to be light colored, which makes them easier to see in the dark of night. Often, these flowers produce sweet, rich fragrances, which also help pollinators find them in the dark.

Other flowers produce scents that aren't very pleasant. Flies that usually consume dead and decaying animals pollinate a type of flower in Southeast Asia called *Rafflesia*. How does it attract these flies? It produces a scent similar to—can you guess?—rotten meat.

***Rafflesia* is the world's largest flower. It can grow as large as a meter across and weigh 11 kilograms.**

The foul smell of this titan arum attracts certain pollinators.

Like a Lock and Key

Some flowers and their pollinators have such a close relationship that their structures fit together almost perfectly. A Hawaiian bird called the I'iwi, for example, has a bill that's perfectly curved to fit inside a similarly shaped flower.

Hawaiian I'iwi bird

An insect in Africa called the mega-nosed fly truly lives up to its name. Like many insects, it sips nectar with a straw-like structure called a *proboscis*. But its proboscis can grow to 10 centimeters long.

The fly uses this long proboscis to reach nectar in very long flowers, where the nectar is out of reach for most other insects.

mega-nosed fly

Structures Help Pollination

Structures on both flowers and their pollinators ensure that pollen moves from flower to flower.

The structure, scent, and bright colors of a flower help ensure that the pollinators find it as they search for nectar. Then, the pollen on the animal's body rubs off on the pistil and stigma, the female organs on the flower where seeds are formed.

Do you remember how fuzzy a bumblebee is? The bee's fuzzy body gets pollen on it as it crawls inside a flower. Some of this pollen rubs off as the bee visits more flowers.

Some flowers, like those pollinated by birds and bats, have leaves and petals that are curved away from the flower's center. This helps the animal fit its head inside the flower without first knocking off any pollen that landed on its fur, feathers, or beak.

lesser long-nosed bat

Sinema globosa spider

swordtail butterfly

ruby-tailed wasp

Think About It

Some plants have only one type of animal that pollinates their flowers. How might this relationship cause problems for the plant? Which of the following is correct?

1. If the animal population increases, the plant will not make any seeds.
2. If the number of animals available to pollinate the flower decreases, the plant may have difficulty producing seeds.
3. If the number of animals increases, the plant will not be able to reproduce.
4. If the animal population decreases, there will be more seeds.

The bee orchid is pollinated by only one type of insect.

Ms. Brown works with students at Awbury Arboretum.

Biography
Meet Ms. Linda Brown

Linda Brown is a horticulturist. A horticulturist is a person who studies and grows plants, flowers, fruits, and vegetables. Ms. Brown works at Awbury Arboretum in Philadelphia.

An arboretum is a place where trees, plants, flowers, and other living things are grown. An arboretum is like a giant garden. Arboretums are places where people can learn a lot about nature.

Pollination

The arboretum is home to many types of flowers. Some of Ms. Brown's favorite flowers are the perennials. Perennials are plants that bloom every year. Some of these flowers are able to survive because of small insects like bees.

Bees are attracted to flowers. Bees get food from flowers. While getting their food, bees also get pollen from the flowers on their legs and bodies. Pollen is a powdery dust produced by plants.

Bees fly to other plants with the pollen on their legs and bodies. The pollen from one plant is then transferred to another plant. From this action, new seeds will grow. New plants grow from seeds.

This bee is on a black-eyed susan.

Sharing Nature

Ms. Brown likes to show people parts of nature that they might never have noticed before. She also knows that the more people learn about nature, the more they will take care of the environment. She says, "Have respect for nature."

Tools of the Trade

With pruning shears, horticulturists trim plants to keep them healthy.

pruning shears

With a gardening spade and fork, horticulturists dig holes for planting or moving plants.

gardening spade and fork

Plant Life Cycles

You have been watching your *Brassica* plants for several weeks now. You've recorded a lot of data about your plants in your Science Notebook.

How can you make a summary of the data? How can you compare your data with your classmates' data?

When scientists want to study or compare data, they sometimes organize that data into graphs. A graph is a diagram that shows relationships between sets of data. For example, you can make a graph that shows how a plant's height changed each week.

In this lesson, you'll work in a group to use data and make graphs.

Graphs help explain the meaning of your data.

Focus

Types of Graphs

A **graph** is a drawing that shows how bits of information relate to each other. Graphs can be helpful tools to show information that is difficult to explain. You can use a graph to show how the temperature changes from winter to spring, to show which kinds of pets are the most common among your classmates, or to show how much taller you have grown in a year.

In this lesson, you will use a graph called a bar graph, shown on the next page, to display the changes in plant height over time. You will learn more about bar graphs and several other types of graphs.

Graphs can help make a point. This kind of graph is a line graph.

Bar graphs show data so it's easy and quick to read.

More About Graphs

Most graphs use bars, lines, or pictures to show data. All graphs should have labels that tell you what kinds of data they represent. In fact, you should be able to look at a graph and tell someone what the graph shows, based on the information in the graph.

A bar graph uses the height of bars to represent data. A bar graph is made of several parts: a horizontal line or axis, a vertical line or axis, and bars drawn up and down.

Making Bar Graphs

Let's imagine you wanted to make a bar graph to show the height of each plant in your group. First, you and the members of your group would need to measure your plants and record the heights in your Science Notebook. Next, you would share your data and write down the height of each plant in the group.

1. Label the **vertical axis** "Height."
2. Add evenly spaced horizontal lines along the vertical axis to represent centimeters. Label the lines 2 cm, 4 cm, 6 cm, and so on.
3. Then label the **horizontal axis** with the name of each student whose plant is being measured.
4. Above each student's name, draw a bar that lines up with the height of that student's plant (indicated by the centimeter lines marked on the vertical axis).

One last step—think of a good title for your graph.

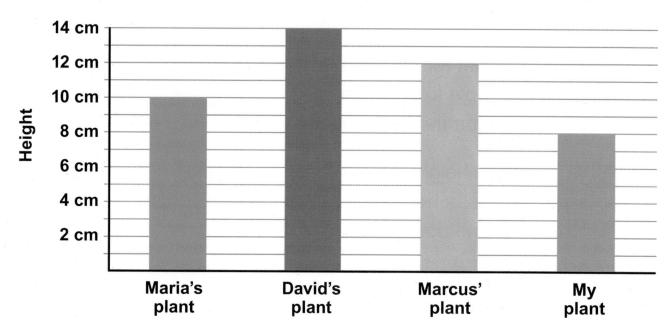

Height of Students' Plants

Line Graphs

Bar graphs work well for showing individual points of data. For example, how tall is each plant in the class? How tall is each person in your class?

But what if you want to know how your plant's height changes over time?

Line graphs work well for showing data that changes over time. Like a bar graph, a line graph has a horizontal axis and a vertical axis. Instead of using bars to show information, a line graph uses a line to connect points of data.

Many science presentations include line graphs.

Determining Growth

A forester might want to know how much an oak tree grew in 6 years. A line graph can show the answer to this question.

Let's imagine the forester has been recording the height of an oak tree on the same day every year. By setting up a line graph with height on the vertical axis, and years on the horizontal axis, the forester can see how fast the tree grew. The graph below shows this information for an oak tree.

A line graph could also show how your plant grows over time as you measure and record its height each day.

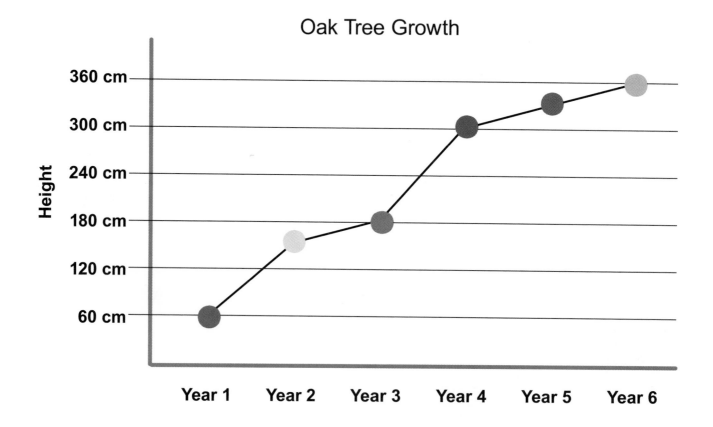

Circle Graphs

A circle graph shows how all the data fills up a circle. Sometimes people call this kind of graph a pie graph or pie chart, because it looks like a pie cut into slices.

Imagine you and your classmates planted seeds of pea plants many weeks ago. Today, all your plants have flowers. Half the plants have pink flowers, one-fourth of the plants have purple flowers, and one-fourth have yellow flowers. How can we show all the colors of these flowers in a circle graph?

The pie chart is titled "Colors of the Flowers." The line down the middle of the circle divides the circle in half. Another line divides one of the halves in half again.

This circle graph shows that half the pea plants have pink flowers. It also shows that one-fourth of the flowers are purple and the remaining one-fourth of the flowers are yellow.

Colors of the Flowers

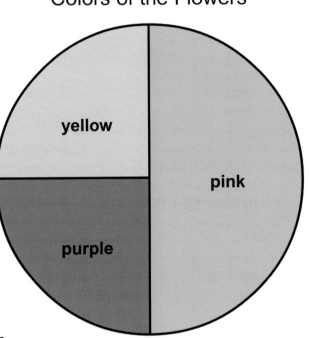

Pictographs

A pictograph uses pictures to represent amounts. Let's imagine you wanted to make a pictograph showing how many leaves are on each plant in your group.

First, you need to know how many leaves are on each plant. Imagine your plant has 14 leaves, Nigel's plant has 10 leaves, Lisa's plant has 12 leaves, and Jose's plant has 15 leaves.

Number of Leaves on My Group's Plants

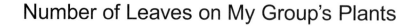

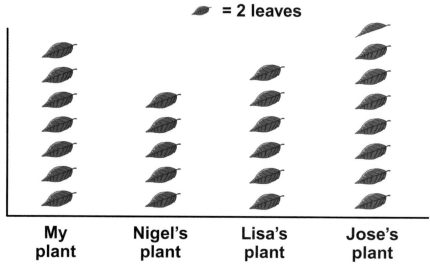

Each person's plant is identified along the horizontal line. A picture represents data. On this pictograph, one leaf on the graph represents two leaves on the plant. The legend is at the top of the graph.

Above each name, there are leaves, one above the other, that represent the data for each person's plant. Remember, one leaf on the graph represents two leaves on the plant. Half of two is one, so a half-leaf on the graph represents one leaf on the plant.

Think About It

Which of the graphs below shows one plant growing taller over time?

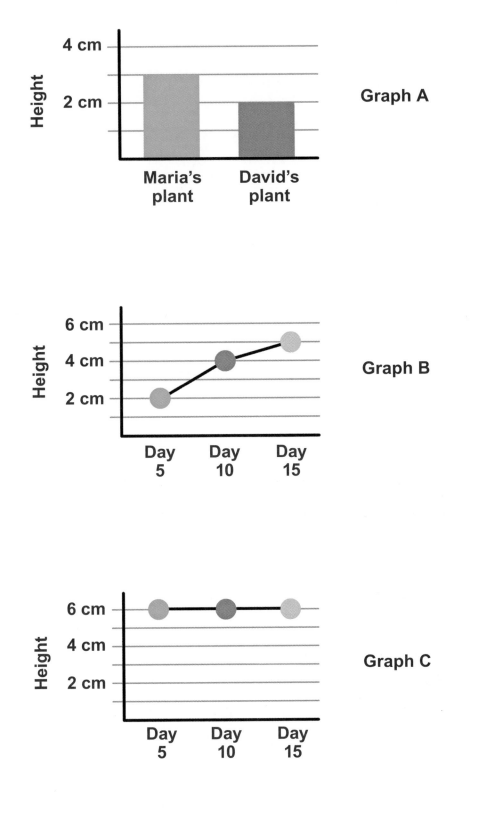

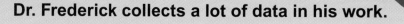

Dr. Frederick collects a lot of data in his work.

Biography
Meet Dr. Lafayette Frederick

Dr. Lafayette Frederick is a plant pathologist. A plant pathologist is someone who studies diseases in plants. Dr. Frederick is like a doctor for plants.

Dr. Frederick makes careful observations and records what he sees in a science journal or notebook. He records data about the size, shape, color, texture, and growth of different parts of plants. Dr. Frederick uses the data to make charts and graphs about different plants.

Fun with Fungi

Dr. Frederick works in Washington, D.C. He studies plants in the laboratory and in nature. He often studies different types of fungi. Fungi are organisms such as mushrooms and molds.

Dr. Frederick studies many things about fungi. He studies types of fungi that are helpful, such as yeast that helps make bread and mold that can be used in medicines. He also studies types of fungi that can be dangerous, such as molds that harm trees and crops.

This slime mold was collected by Dr. Frederick.

Dr. Frederick studies molds like this under a microscope.

This honey fungus is among those studied by Dr. Frederick.

Learning from Charts and Graphs

Charts and graphs are important tools for scientists like Dr. Frederick. Charts and graphs can show the data from a science journal or a notebook. For example, Dr. Frederick can create a chart that shows how tall a plant grows over several days or weeks.

Charts and graphs also help scientists understand plant life cycles. Charts and graphs let Dr. Frederick know if a plant is growing normally or if its growth is unusual. Charts and graphs also let Dr. Frederick share his data with other scientists. Dr. Frederick says, "Organizing observations and information into tables and graphs is very helpful and useful."

Samples of Dr. Frederick's notes

Experience

Different Views of Data

Materials

Brassica plants

pencil

colored pencils or crayons

metric ruler

Blank Graph sheets

You have seen how graphs help us share information. Try creating your own graphs. Look at the data in your Science Notebook. Measure your plants now. Add that information to the data in your Science Notebook.

Work with your group to record the data on the two graph sheets provided by the teacher.

Procedures

1. Look at the data in your Science Notebook.
2. Look at the Blank Graph sheets. You will use these to make your bar graphs.
3. One graph is to show the differences between Brassica plants.
4. One graph is to show how one Brassica plant from the group has grown over time.

students creating graphs

5. Use a ruler to make straight lines for the bars.
6. Check your numbers. The data must be correct. Ask another student to review your work. The graph must be clear to others.

After you finish each graph, write three statements that tell about the information in the graph. Put these sentences on the back of the graph paper. Remember to write your name on each sheet.

Experience

Planning a Presentation

Sharing information is an important part of science. We can share information in many different ways. We share through words, stories, drawings, models, computer displays, songs, poems, movement, games, and more.

Talk with your group about your plant life cycle group presentation. Take notes. On the Presentation Planner sheet, write what each group member will do to prepare for the **presentation**. Group members will make life cycle cards and other display materials. It's a team effort, so everyone participates. Get ready to do a great job.

Working together is important.

Careful planning will result in a good presentation.

Experience

Planning Together

Today is planning day. You'll finish up your life cycle cards and any other visual display material you plan to use.

You'll also plan what you want to say during your presentation.

Experience

Group Presentations

Today is oral presentation day.

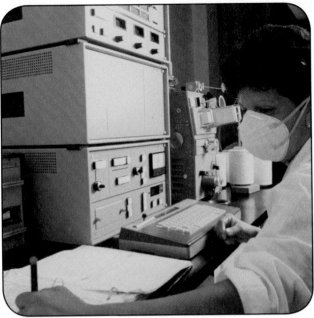
Researcher recording data

Scientist analyzing data

Checkpoint
Review

When you think about science, you probably think about exploration and discovery. Hands-on investigations give us a chance to find out more about the world around us.

Another way we learn is through books, pictures, films, and presentations. If we share what we know, we help others learn along with us.

Think about your observations and investigations during our lessons about plants. Write some of your thoughts in your Science Notebook. We call this *reflection* or thinking about your experiences.

Pick the Insect

Which of these animals is an insect?

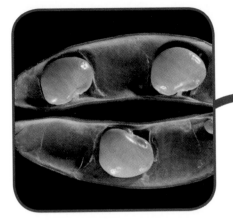

Patterns

Scientists sometimes talk about patterns and cycles in nature that repeat. How is the plant life cycle an example of a pattern that repeats?

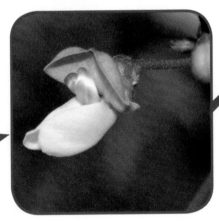

The cycle flows from seed to sprout to seedling to flower, and finally to fruit.

What's Missing?

Look at the graph below. What information is missing?

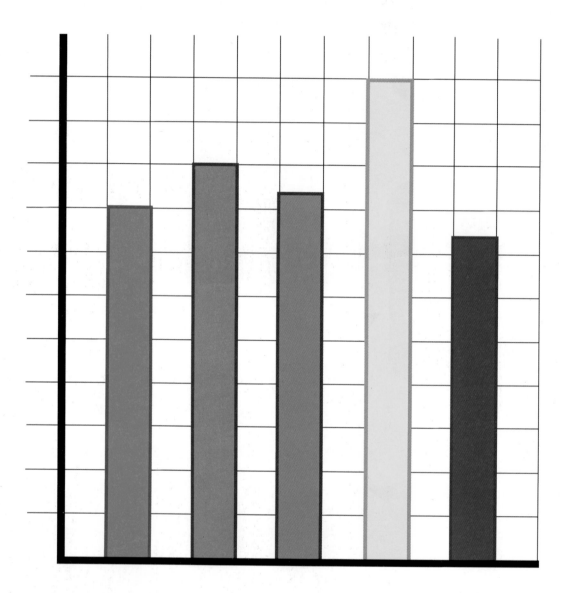

What kind of information is needed to complete this graph?

Data Is Important

You've learned about plant life cycles—how plants develop from seeds, grow stems, produce leaves, and make flowers and seeds. This pattern repeats in every generation.

Like plants, other living organisms—including people—have patterns in their life cycles. People begin life as babies who depend on their parents to meet their needs. Babies grow into children, develop into teenagers, and later become adults. Like plants, their bodies continue to change and grow. Other animals follow a similar cycle.

In this lesson, you'll observe and compare the life cycles, needs, and growth of plants and of a group of people—your fellow classmates. You also will learn about the needs shared by plants, animals, and other organisms. Finally, you will practice presenting data to your classmates.

Studying the life cycle of plants can be very rewarding.

Experience

How Do Plants and People Compare?

We have been studying plants and watching them grow. As you know, plants need water to grow and develop. Without water, seeds will not germinate. Water also helps deliver food and minerals throughout a plant. Without any water, plants would die.

How about you? What would happen to you if you did not have water to drink? First, you would get thirsty. Then, you would become **dehydrated**. People need water to stay healthy.

Plants are living things. Animals are living things. And living things need water. What else do living things need?

Work with a partner to make a list of what plants and animals need. Complete a **Venn diagram** to show your ideas.

studying plants

taking care of plants

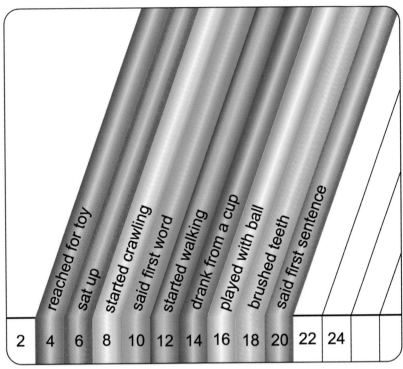

Time Line of Child Development

reached for toy
sat up
started crawling
said first word
started walking
drank from a cup
played with ball
brushed teeth
said first sentence

2 4 6 8 10 12 14 16 18 20 22 24

Age of Child in Months

This time line shows almost two years of a child's life.

Experience

Recording Data and Changes

Plants and people develop differently. We can construct graphs and **time lines** to show these patterns of change.

When you were born, someone checked your height and weight. He or she recorded the data. Each time you went to the doctor for a checkup, someone wrote down your height and weight. You might have seen a graph that showed these changes over time. Graphs show data in a way that lets us see patterns.

As babies and children get older, they change. Most babies begin to walk about the time of their first birthday. Later they learn how to run and go up and down stairs. You could make a time line to record these events. A time line shows changes or specific events that occur over a period of time.

Focus

What Plants Need

You've watched your *Brassica* plants develop from the day they were tiny seeds that you planted in the soil. You've taken care of them by watering them, and by thinning and transplanting the plants when their containers became too crowded.

You have learned a lot about the needs of plants by raising your *Brassica* plants. Let's review what plants need.

Like all organisms, plants need water, air, food, and **habitat**. But not all plants are lucky enough to have someone like you to take care of them! How do other plants find water, food, air, and habitat?

Watching plants grow

Plants Make Their Own Food

Plants don't eat food the way animals do. Plants don't have a mouth, a stomach, or any of the organs we have that help us break down our food.

Instead, plants make their own food. They make food using water, a gas in air called carbon dioxide, and sunlight. Plants use energy from the sun to turn carbon dioxide and water into food for the plant. Plants use this food to provide the energy they need to grow and reproduce.

With sunlight, air, and water, plants make their own food.

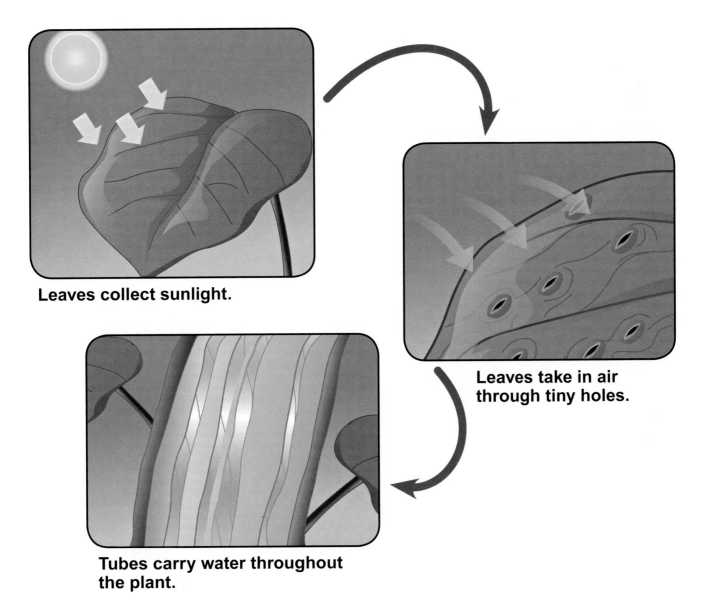

Leaves collect sunlight.

Leaves take in air through tiny holes.

Tubes carry water throughout the plant.

Plants Are Planted

As you learned before, plants have special structures that help them stay alive. Their roots absorb water and nutrients from the soil. Their leaves collect the sun's energy and produce food. Air also enters the plant through tiny holes in the leaves.

Where the acorn falls...

Plants can't move from one habitat to another the way animals can. When a seed lands on the ground and germinates, that spot becomes the plant's new home. Because it can make its own food and absorb water from the ground, a plant can provide for itself even when anchored in one place.

...the oak tree grows.

You Are What You Eat

Animals share the same basic needs as plants: air, water, food, and habitat. But animals must eat food—no animal can produce its own food the way plants can.

Animals have many, many ways of finding food. Some animals, called **carnivores,** are meat eaters that eat other animals. You might think of big animals, like lions or sharks, when you think of carnivores. But many smaller animals, like dragonflies, frogs, shrews, and centipedes. are carnivores, too.

Frog eating an insect

Fish eating a smaller fish

Owl eating a caterpillar

Crane feeding a chick

Cat eating a mouse

Mongoose eating a mussel

rabbit

cow

rhinoceros

giraffe

orangutan

caterpillar

Herbivores and Omnivores

Animals that eat only plants or plant parts are called **herbivores**. Many different types of animals are herbivores. Rabbits, many types of birds, insects, horses, and even rhinoceroses are herbivores. They eat leaves, stems, fruits, or seeds. Several herbivores are shown here.

Some animals, including people, are called **omnivores**, which means they can eat both plants and animals.

How Animals Find Food and Water

Most animals, herbivores and carnivores alike, can move about in search of food and water in the environment. They may hunt, graze, or even set traps, like spiderwebs.

Elephants travel to water holes.

When you are hungry or thirsty, you probably don't go outside and hunt for prey, nibble on the lawn, or drink from a pond. In our society, we buy most of our food from grocery stores or markets. Water is often supplied to our homes.

People can carry water with them.

But, like animals, we also depend on the environment to provide us with these resources. Our food comes from farms, where crops grow in the soil. Some of those crops feed livestock, like cows and chickens. Our water comes from lakes and rivers, just like the water animals drink. We breathe the same air other animals do, and sometimes even build our homes in the same places where animals live.

Wild animals hunt for their food.

Most people shop for their food.

Fly agaric mushrooms are poisonous.

Mold on a strawberry spoils it.

Blewit mushrooms are edible.

Mold makes blue cheese taste good.

Fungi and Bacteria

As you might know, not all organisms can be classified as plants or animals. You may have heard of other types of organisms, such as bacteria or fungi. Bacteria are tiny organisms. Fungi are a diverse group of organisms, including mushrooms, molds, and yeasts.

Like us, bacteria and fungi need a source of food, water, air, and habitat. But fungi and bacteria often find these in places where we would never even look.

Bad and Good Bacteria

Sometimes, bacteria and fungi use our own bodies to provide for their needs. When these organisms make a home in our bodies, they can make us ill. Strep throat and ear infections, for example, are illnesses caused by bacteria that invade our bodies in search of a home.

Bacteria and fungi aren't always harmful. They play many important roles in our lives. For example, bacteria are helpful in digesting food. A special type of fungus called yeast is used in making bread.

Bacteria and fungi are important to the environment, too. Many bacteria and fungi live in soil, where they eat dead and decaying plants and animals. If they were not there, what do you think might happen in our forests?

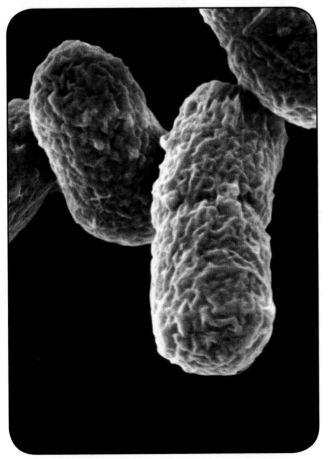

E. coli bacteria can cause illness.

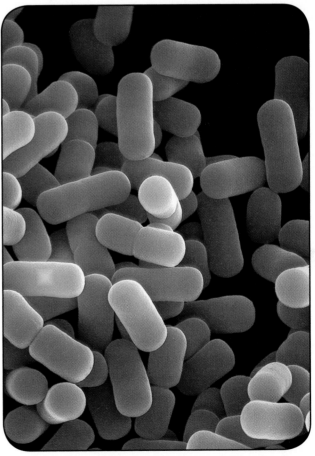

These are healthful yogurt bacteria.

Diagram It

Think about how carnivores and herbivores are alike and different.

Look at the pictures on this page. Which do you think are carnivores and which are herbivores?

Organize your ideas into a Venn diagram showing the similarities and differences between carnivores and herbivores.

great white shark

gray wolf

moose

giant panda

These scientists are collecting data about plants.

Reviewing Data Collected

Over the past few weeks you have observed and recorded data about plants. You have had a close-up view of how plants grow and change. You found out what plants need to stay alive. Then, you compared the needs of plants and people.

Your next job is to summarize the data. That is, you will write down the main points, using the data you have gathered. This step will help you prepare to share the information with your classmates.

You Are a Star Presenter

Lights, camera, action! Your group will make a presentation about plant growth and development. When we communicate with others, we all learn from the experience. Remember to speak clearly, look at the audience, and show your interest in the subject. That will get you off to a great start.

Many presenters stand while speaking.

Speakers sometimes sit to give a presentation.

Checkpoint

Review

Based on what they are eating, which one of the photographs below shows a carnivore?

tortoise

deer

spider

elephant

porcupine

goat

Plants and people need many of the same things to live and grow.

Compare and Contrast

Compare and contrast your needs as a person with the needs of a plant. Which needs are the same? Which needs are different?

Tables of Measure

Length

Metric System	English System
1 centimeter (cm) = 10 millimeters (mm)	1 foot (ft) = 12 inches (in.)
1 decimeter (dm) = 10 centimeters (cm)	1 yard (yd) = 36 inches (in.)
1 meter (m) = 10 decimeters (dm)	1 yard (yd) = 3 feet (ft)
1 meter (m) = 100 centimeters (cm)	1 rod (rd) = 16 ½ feet (ft)
1 decameter (dam) = 10 meters (m)	1 mile (mi) = 5280 feet (ft)
1 kilometer (km) = 1000 meters (m)	1 mile (mi) = 1760 yards (yd)

Weight (Mass)

Metric System	English System
1 gram (g) = 1000 milligrams (mg)	1 pound (lb) = 16 ounces (oz)
1 kilogram (kg) = 1000 grams (g)	1 ton (T) = 2000 pounds (lb)
1 metric ton (t) = 1000 kilograms (kg)	

Capacity

Metric System	English System
1 liter (L) = 1000 milliliters (mL)	1 pint (pt) = 2 cups (c)
1 decaliter (daL) = 10 liters (L)	1 quart (qt) = 2 pints (pt)
1 kiloliter (kL) = 1000 liters (L)	1 gallon (gal) = 4 quarts (qt)
	1 peck (pk) = 8 quarts (qt)
	1 bushel (bu) = 4 pecks (pk)

Useful Measurement Equivalents

Length
1 inch = 2.54 centimeters
1 foot = 12 inches = 30.48 centimeters
1 yard = 3 feet = 36 inches = 91.44 centimeters

Weight (mass)
1 oz = 28.35 grams
1 pound = 16 ounces = 453.59 grams
1 ton = 2000 pounds = 907 kilograms

Volume
1 quart (liquid) = 2 pints = 32 fluid ounces = 946 milliliters (0.946 liter)

Rulers You Can Use

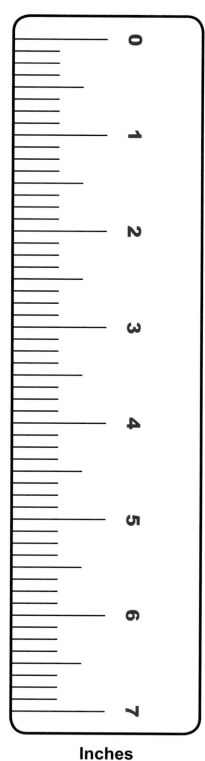

Inches

English System

Centimeters

Metric System

Steps in the Scientific Method

Scientific method is a process that scientists follow to explore and find answers to questions.

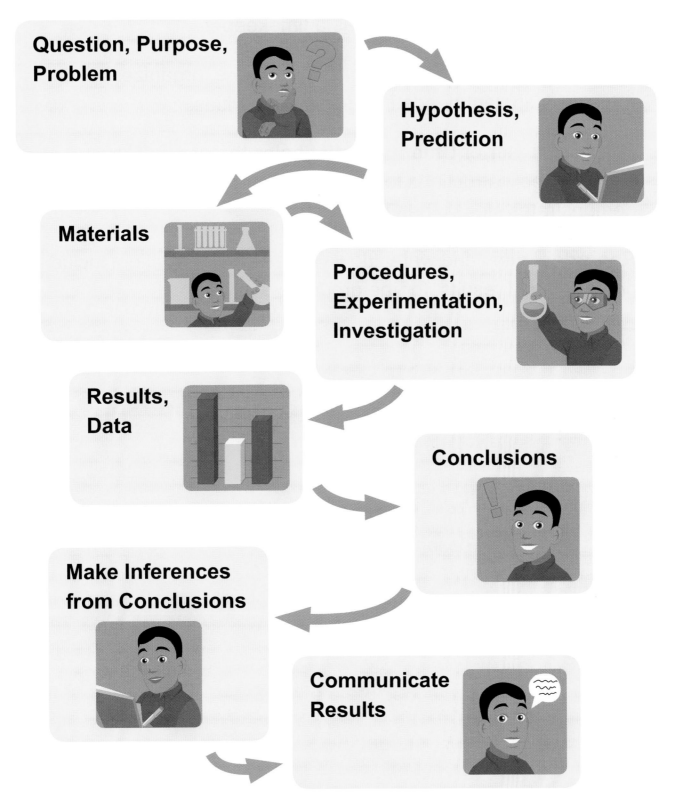

Suggested Roles for Students in Cooperative Groups

- **Group Leader** maintains order, keeps efforts focused, facilitates cooperative work, and serves as a timekeeper.

- **Equipment and Materials Manager** gathers, organizes, and returns equipment needed for specific activities.

- **Chief Engineer** or **Chief Scientist** helps the group follow step-by-step instructions for construction activities and demonstrates steps when necessary.

- **Recorder** keeps and writes down important information, including decisions and results, for the group.

Self-Assessment Checklist for Group Work

☐ I remembered my special job (or role).

☐ I was a careful observer.

☐ I followed directions.

☐ I listened to my teammates.

☐ I participated in group discussions.

☐ I was polite and considerate of others.

☐ I completed the work and helped clean up.

Careers in Science

- **Astronomer** – studies the stars, planets, and other heavenly bodies

- **Biochemist** – studies cells to determine the life processes of cells and entire organisms

- **Biologist** – studies life processes of plants and animals

- **Botanist** – studies plants

- **Chemist** – studies the make-up and properties of substances and how they react with one another

- **Civil Engineer** – designs highways, bridges, tunnels, waterworks, harbors, and so on

- **Computer Scientist** – studies and applies computer programming

- **Electrical Engineer** – applies the technology of electricity to the design and operation of equipment

- **Entomologist** – studies insects

- **Geologist** – studies the structure and history of Earth

- **Laboratory Technician** – performs laboratory processes, tests, experiments, and so on

- **Medical Doctor** – practices medicine to treat sickness, injury, and disease

- **Meteorologist** – studies the atmosphere and weather conditions

- **Nurse** – takes care of sick and injured people

- **Oceanographer** – studies the physical properties of the ocean

- **Zoologist** – studies animals

Sample Graphs

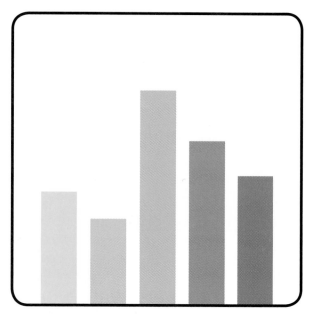

Bar graph

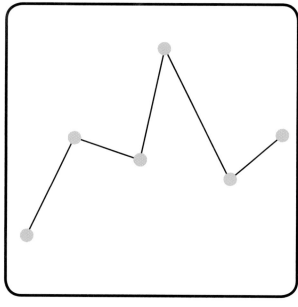

Line graph

Pictograph

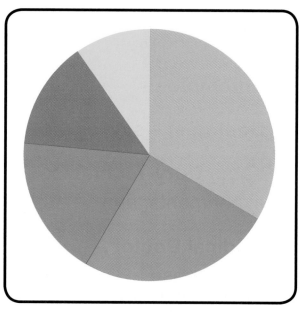

Pie graph

Six Major Groups of Living Things

Animals

Plants

Fungi

**Protozoa and Algae
(protists)**

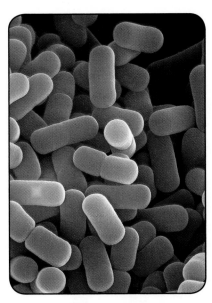
Bacteria

**Extreme Bacteria
(archaebacteria)**

Our World

Living Things

Nonliving Things

Pronunciation Guide

The table below provides sample words to explain the sounds associated with specific letters and letter combinations used in the respellings in this book. For example, *a* represents the short "a" sound in *cat*, while *ay* represents the long "a" sound in *day*. Letter combinations are used to approximate certain more complex sounds. For example, in the respelling of *Celsius*—SEL-see-uhs—the letters *uhs* represent the vowel sound you hear in *shut* and *other*.

Vowels

a	short a: **a**pple, c**a**t
ay	long a: c**a**ne, d**ay**
e, eh	short e: h**e**n, b**e**d
ee	long e: f**ee**d, t**ea**m
i, ih	short i: l**i**p, act**i**ve
iy	long i: tr**y**, m**igh**t
ah	short o: h**o**t, f**a**ther
oh	long o: h**o**me, thr**ow**
uh	short u: sh**u**t, **o**ther
yoo	long u: **u**nion, c**u**te

Letter Combinations

ch	**ch**in, an**c**ient
sh	**sh**ow, mi**ss**ion
zh	vi**s**ion, a**z**ure
th	**th**in, heal**th**
th	**th**en, hea**th**er
ur	b**ir**d, f**ur**ther, w**or**d
us	b**us**, cr**us**t
or	c**our**t, f**or**mal
ehr	**err**or, c**are**
oo	c**oo**l, tr**ue**, f**ew**, r**u**le
ow	n**ow**, **ou**t
ou	l**oo**k, p**u**ll, w**ou**ld
oy	c**oi**n, t**oy**
aw	s**aw**, m**au**l, f**a**ll
ng	so**ng**, fi**ng**er
air	**A**ristotle, b**a**rrister
ahr	c**a**rt, m**a**rtyr

Consonants

b	**b**utter, **b**aby
d	**d**og, cra**d**le
f	**f**un, **ph**one
g	**g**rade, an**g**le
h	**h**at, a**h**ead
j	**j**u**dg**e, **g**or**g**e
k	**k**ite, **c**ar, bla**ck**
l	**l**ily, mi**l**e
m	**m**om, ca**m**el
n	**n**ext, ca**n**did
p	**p**rice, co**pp**er
r	**r**ubber, f**r**ee
s	**s**mall, **c**ircle, ha**ss**le
t	**t**on, po**tt**ery
v	**v**ase, **v**i**v**id
w	**w**all, a**w**ay
y	**y**ellow, ka**y**ak
z	**z**ebra, ha**z**e

Glossary

abdomen: the last section of an insect's body

antennae: sensors, used for feeling and smelling, that are located on an insect's head

arboretum: a place where trees, shrubs, and other plants are grown for people to study and enjoy

bacteria: a kind of very tiny, or microscopic, organism

botanist: a person who studies plants

carnivore: an animal that feeds on other animals

compound eyes: the complex eyes of some insects; made of more than one simple lens

crop rotation: to change the crops growing in a particular area from one growing season to another

dehydrated: to not have enough water and be dried out

ecologist: a person who studies the relationships among plants and animals and their environment

embryo: the tiny plant inside a seed

environment: the nonliving and living factors that affect an organism

exoskeleton: the hard outer covering of an insect

fertilizer: special food to help plants grow better and produce more fruit

flower: the part of a plant that produces fruit

fruit: the part of a plant that contains the seeds

fungus: molds, rust, mushrooms, and similar organisms

germinate: to break out of the seed coat

graph: a diagram that shows a relationship among two or more groups of numbers or drawings

greenhouse: a building made of glass or plastic in which plants can grow and be protected from the weather

habitat: the place where a plant or an animal can live and grow

head: the first section of an insect's body, to which its antennae are attached

herbivore: an animal that feeds on plants

horizontal axis: the horizontal line on a graph

horticulturist: a person who studies and grows plants

interdependence: the idea that all living things need each other

leaf: a plant organ that helps make food for the plant

life cycle: the series of changes a living thing goes through in its lifetime

naturalist: a person who studies plants and animals

nectar: the sugary liquid inside a flower that bees and other animals use for food

nectar guides: special color patterns on some flowers to direct certain pollinators to nectar

nutrient: any substance that provides food that plants need to stay strong and healthy

omnivore: an animal that feeds on both plants and animals

organ: a plant part that does a special job within a plant system

organism: any living thing, plant or animal

perennial: plants that last for several years and bloom year after year

petal: leaf-shaped structure around the inner parts of a flower

presentation: sharing research and information with other students

pistil: the female part of a flower, which can develop into a fruit and produce seeds

pollen: a fine powder at the end of a flower's stamens that is involved in fertilization

pollination: the transfer of pollen from one flower's stamens to the top of another flower's pistil

pollinator: an animal that moves pollen from one flower to another

proboscis: a long, flexible snout of an insect, used for sucking

reproduce: to make new living things of the same kind

root: the underground plant organ that keeps a plant in place and helps it get food and water

seed: the part of a plant that can grow into a new plant

seed leaves: the leaves of the plant embryo, inside a seed coat

sepal: the outermost part of a flower, which covers and protects the other parts of the flower inside the bud

stamen: long, thin stalks that produce a flower's pollen

stem: the plant organ that supports a plant and transports water and nutrients

stomata: tiny openings in a leaf that allow gases to pass in and out

summarize: to restate briefly the main points of a text, leaving out minor points

thin: to reduce the number of plants in an area so the remaining plants will have more food, water, and room to grow

thorax: the middle section of an insect's body, to which its wings and legs are attached

time line: a table that lists important events that happen over a period of time

transplant: to move a plant from one area to another

true leaves: leaves produced by the seedling or more mature plant

Venn diagram: a diagram that uses overlapping circles to show relationships

vertical axis: the vertical line on a graph

Illustrations Credits

Key: t=top; b=bottom; c=center; l=left; r=right

All artwork: © K12 Inc.

Front cover: © Bob Daemmrich/The Image Works; (background) © VStock, LLC/Index Stock.

Back cover: (t) © Bruce Coleman, Inc./Alamy; (b) © Lynwood M. Chace/Photo Researchers, Inc.

Introduction: © Digital Archive Japan/Alamy

Lesson 1: 3 © Robert Maass/Corbis. **4** (t) © Holt Studios International Ltd./Alamy; (b) © Stone/Getty Images. **5** © Brand X Pictures/Jupiterimages. **6** © K12 Inc. **7** © Dwight Kuhn. **8** © Vaughan Fleming/Photo Researchers, Inc. **9** (both) © Dwight Kuhn. **10** © Roger Phillips/Dorling Kindersley. **11** (tl) © Design Pics Inc./Alamy; (tr) © Patti Murray/Animals Animals/Earth Scenes; (cl) © Nigel Cattlin/Photo Researchers, Inc.; (cr) © ALIX/Photo Researchers, Inc.; (bl) © Geoff Bryant/Photo Researchers, Inc.; (br) © Geoff Bryant/Photo Researchers, Inc. **12** (l) © Michael P. Gadomski/Photo Researchers, Inc.; (c) © Pressebildagentur/Alamy; (r) © Dwight Kuhn. **13** © Papilio/Alamy. **14,15,16** © The International Canopy Network. **17** © Gary Braasch. **18** (both) © Photo Objects.net. **19** © Marmotta PhotoArt/Photograhers Direct. **20** © Biophoto Associates/Photo Researchers, Inc.; (inset) © Dr. Stanley Flegler/Visuals Unlimited.

Lesson 2: 21 © Lynda Richardson/Corbis. **22** (tl) © Harry Giglio/NonStock/Jupiterimages; (tr) © Comstock Images/Jupiterimages; (c) © photolibrary/Index Stock; (b) © photolibrary/Index Stock. **23** (t) © Jerome Wexler/Photo Researchers, Inc.; (b) © Dwight Kuhn.

Lesson 3: 27 © Lynda Richardson/Corbis. **28** © Glenda Kapsalis/Photographers Direct. **31** © Corbis; (inset) © Bettmann/Corbis. **32,33** © Bettmann/Corbis. **34** © Plainpicture/Alamy; (inset) © imagebroker/ Alamy. **35** © Bettmann/Corbis. **36** © Chris Sattlberger/Photo Researchers, Inc.; (inset) © Kenneth W. Fink/Photo Researchers, Inc. **37** © USDA/Nature Source/Photo Researchers, Inc. **38** (tl)(br) © Photodisc; (tr) © Eyewire; (bl) © Photo Objects.net. **39** © Bettmann/Corbis. **40** (all) From the Wisconsin Fast Plants Growing Instructions, used with permission, © 2001 Carolina Biological Supply Company. **41** (tl) © Jerome Wexler/Photo Researchers, Inc.; (cr)(br) © Gilbert S. Grant/Photo Researchers, Inc.; (cl)(bc)

© Robert J. Erwin/Photo Researchers, Inc. **42** © Sheila Terry/Photo Researchers, Inc. **43** (tl) © Mark Windom/Index Stock; (tc) © imagebroker/Alamy; (tr) © Jim W. Grace/Photo Researchers, Inc.; (bl) © ALIX/Photo Researchers, Inc.; (bc) © Adam Jones/Photo Researchers, Inc.; (br) © Nigel Cattlin/Photo Researchers, Inc. **44** © Image Alchemy/Alamy. **45** © Mica/Alamy. **46** (tl) © Ken Wagner/Phototake; (bl) © Barbara K. Hesse/Visuals Unlimited; (bc) © Dr. Jeremy Burgess/Photo Researchers, Inc.; (br) © William Ormerod/Visuals Unlimited. **47** © VStock, LLC/Index Stock. **48** © Hunt Institute for Botanical Documentation, Carnegie Mellon University. **50** (t) © I. Glory/Alamy; (c) © Steve Austin/Papilio/Corbis; (b) © Biophoto Associates/Photo Researchers, Inc. **51** (all) From the Wisconsin Fast Plants Growing Instructions, used with permission, © 2001 Carolina Biological Supply Company. **52** © K12 Inc. **53** © Gail Jankus/Photo Researchers, Inc.

Lesson 4: 55 © Brand X Pictures/Alamy. **56** © K12 Inc. **57** (tl) © IT Stock; (tr) © Jerome Wexler/Visuals Unlimited; (bl) © Creatas Images/Jupiterimages; (br) © Karl Maslowski/Photo Researchers, Inc. **58** © Artville. **59** (both) © K12 Inc. **60** © Westend61/Alamy. **61** (t) © WildPictures/Alamy; (bl) © Paul Wood/Alamy; (br) © blickwinkel/Alamy. **62** (both) © Edward Parker/Alamy. **63** (t) © Darwin Dale/Photo Researchers, Inc; (c) © Bruce Coleman, Inc./Alamy; (b) © Natural Selection/Creatas Images/Jupiterimages. **64** © Roger Eritja/Alamy. **65** (l) © Able Stock/Index Stock; (r) © Steve Bloom Images/Alamy. **66** (l) © Kjell B. Sandved/Photo Researchers, Inc.; (r) © Frank Walker/Alamy. **67** (t) © Jack Jeffrey/Photo Resource Hawaii; (b) © Michael and Patricia Fogden. **68** (l) © WildPictures/Alamy; (cl) © Bob Jensen/Alamy; (cr) © Roger Eritja/Alamy; (r) © Dr. Merlin Tuttle/ BCI /Photo Researchers, Inc. **69** © Nuridsany et Perrenou/Photo Researchers, Inc. **70** (both) © Courtesy of Linda Brown/Awbury Arboretum. **71** © Trevor Smithers /ARPS/Alamy. **72** (t) © Photo Objects.net; (b) © Able Stock/Index Stock.

Lesson 5: 73 © Lawrence Migdale. **74,75,77** © Photos.com Select/Index Stock. **82** © Courtesy of Lafayette Frederick; (inset) © Jason Varney Photography. **83** (t) © Courtesy of Lafayette Frederick; (b) © Micro Discovery/Corbis; (b) © IT Stock. **84** © Courtesy of Lafayette Frederick. **85** © Jeremy Horner/Corbis. **86** © Photo Network/Alamy. **87** © Image Source/

Alamy. **88** © Photo Network/Alamy. **89** (l) © Royalty-Free/Corbis; (r) © Roger Ressmeyer/Corbis. **90** (all) © IT Stock. **91** (tl) © Jerome Wexler/Photo Researchers, Inc.; (tr)(br) © Gilbert S. Grant/Photo Researchers, Inc.; (bl)(cr) © Robert J. Erwin/Photo Researchers, Inc.

Lesson 6: 93 © Diana Koenigsberg/Botanica/Jupiterimages. **94** (l) © Janine Wiedel Photolibrary/Alamy; (r) © Jim West Photography/Photographers Direct. **96** © Sally and Richard Greenhill/Alamy. **98** (t) © Dwight Kuhn; (b) © imagebroker/Alamy. **99** (tl)(tr) © Joe McDonald/Corbis; (tc) © John Madere/Corbis; (bl) © Michael & Patricia Fogden/Corbis; (bc) © photolibrary/Index Stock; (br) © Corbis/Jupiterimages. **100** (tl) © Herbert Kehrer/zefa/Corbis; (tc) © VStock, LLC/Index Stock; (tr) © Kevin Schafer/Corbis; (bl) © Keith Levit Photography/Index Stock; (bc) © Frank Lukasseck/zefa/Corbis; (br) © Michael & Patricia Fogden/Corbis. **101** (tr) © Keith Levit Photography/Index Stock; (cl) © Tom Brakefield/zefa/Corbis; (cr) © Royalty-Free/Corbis; (bl) © Don Mason/Corbis. **102** (tl)(bl) © IT Stock; (tr) © Clouds Hill Imaging Ltd./Corbis; (br) © D. Boschung/zefa/Corbis. **103** (l) © Gary Gaugler/Visuals Unlimited; (r) © Dr. Dennis Kunkel/Visuals Unlimited. **104** (tl) © Tim Davis/Corbis; (tr) © Photodisc; (bl) © Charles Krebs/Corbis; (br) © Ralph Reinhold/Index Stock. **105** © Royalty-Free/Corbis. **106** (l) © Comstock Images/Jupiterimages; (r) © Dennis MacDonald/Alamy. **107** (tl) © George D. Lepp/Corbis; (tc) © Photodisc; (tr) © Joe McDonald/Corbis; (bl) © Frank Lukasseck/zefa/Corbis; (bc) © Tom Brakefield/Corbis; (br) © USDA/Nature Source/Photo Researchers, Inc. **108** © Anthony Redpath/Corbis.

Appendix G: (tl) © Dynamic Graphics; (tc) © Photodisc; (tr) © IT Stock; (bl) © Michael Abbey/Visuals Unlimited; (bc) © Dr. Dennis Kunkel/Visuals Unlimited; (br) © Ralph Robinson/Visuals Unlimited.

Appendix H: (t) NASA Goddard Space Flight Center Image by Reto Stöckli. **Living Things** (tl) © Dynamic Graphics; (tc) © Photodisc; (tr) © IT Stock; (bl) © Michael Abbey/Visuals Unlimited; (bc) © Dr. Dennis Kunkel/Visuals Unlimited; (br) © Ralph Robinson/Visuals Unlimited; **Nonliving Things** (tl) © Comstock Images/Punchstock; (tc) © photolibrary/Index Stock; (tr) © Matt Meadows/Peter Arnold, Inc.; (bl) © Dynamic Graphics; (bc) © photolibrary/Index Stock; (br) © Brand X ictures/Jupiterimages.

Index